THE
JOURNEY WITHIN
DREAMS ACROSS BORDERS

Sally Barrilla

Discovering Strength, Growth, and the Power of Self
La Fuerza Por A Dentro

*Written by his daughter,
this is the story of Miguel
Barrilla—a journey of
courage, perseverance, and
a life built from dreams.*

*Escrito por su hija, esta es la historia de
Miguel Barrilla: un viaje de coraje,
perseverancia y una vida construida a partir
de sueños.*

This book is dedicated to everyone who always encouraged me to fight for my dreams, to recognize that writing is powerful, and that you can share your voice and share your story. Thank you to my parents, especially my dad, who I know is so proud to finally have his story shared and written, my grandparents, my aunts, uncles, amazing cousins, and, best of all, to Alex; thank you for always being an amazing support. I love you all.

Contents

1
The Beginning

Our tale begins in the bustling coastal city of Guayaquil, Ecuador. It was May 1975, the sun was high, and the air was thick with salt and anticipation. Two young men, Miguel Barrilla and Guido, stood at the edge of their small world, gazing toward a wide horizon that promised more than their hometown could offer.

They were only nineteen at that time, with their eyes full of hope and minds full of dreams. Their lives stretched out before them like a road untraveled. Both carried little more than a change of clothes, a few crumpled bills in their torn pockets, and a fierce determination to chase the dream whispered in every corner of Latin America—*la vida nueva*—a new life.

Miguel's mother, María Briones, had left Ecuador to build a new life in New York City. At that time, Miguel was just a young boy who saw the American dream from the letters that his mother used to write him. Her letters were filled with stories of tall buildings and bright lights, of opportunity and freedom. Miguel had read each one until the paper began to wear thin, dreaming of the day he would see her again.

"¿Estás listo, Miguelito?" (*Are you ready, Miguelito*) Guido asked, slinging a small bag over his shoulder as the early morning sun painted the empty streets gold.

Miguel nodded as he took a deep breath and released it to calm his pounding heart. "Listo. No hay vuelta atrás ahora" (*Ready. There's no turning back now*).

The first stretch of their journey took them north, from Guayaquil to Colombia. They travelled through dusty border towns and narrow roads that wound between emerald mountains. They traveled mostly by bus, sometimes by foot, and occasionally hitched rides from strangers who asked too many questions. Every passing day of their journey was uncertain, but the two friends were certain about one thing: their destination. They found comfort in laughter and strength in their struggle. Every step taken further made them firmer in their decision.

At one stop, a kind woman handed them tamales wrapped in banana leaves.

"Para la suerte," she said with a smile (*For good luck*).

Miguel thanked her quietly as he tucked the moment away. He saw it as a sign that the world isn't entirely filled with danger and hardship. Even in tough times, there is comfort in hopefulness, better people, and small moments like this.

After days of travel, they reached Bogotá, where the air was cooler and thinner. Nights were long and filled with talk. The two friends would look at each other and whisper, sometimes of dreams, sometimes of fear.

"¿De verdad crees que llegaremos a Estados Unidos?" (*You really think we'll make it to the U.S.*) Guido asked one night, staring at the dim glow of the city lights below their cheap hostel window.

Miguel hesitated before answering, "Tengo que creerlo. Mi madre está ahí. Es razón suficiente" (*I have to believe it. My mother's there. That's enough reason*).

They journeyed onward to the Caribbean coast, reaching Santa Marta and Cartagena, both vibrant cities bursting with color and music. The scent of fried fish and sea breeze mixed with diesel smoke as they navigated crowded ports. In San Andrés Island, they faced a turning point.

Guido began to waver. The uncertainty, the exhaustion, and the whispers of danger that trailed them had begun to weigh on him. One night, under a star-filled sky, Guido finally said the words Miguel's ears dreaded hearing.

"Amigo… No puedo más. Mi casa está en Ecuador. Extraño a mi familia. Esto—esto no es para mi," he gestured toward the endless ocean (*Amigo… I can't keep going. My home is in Ecuador. I miss my family. This—this isn't for me*).

Miguel's heart sank. He wanted to protest, to convince Guido to stay by his side. But instead, he nodded. "Entonces vete a casa, hermano. Yo seguiré por los dos" (*Then go home, brother. I'll keep going for the both of us*).

They clasped hands in silence. Fear had outrun Guido's will, and he had gone back to Ecuador. The next morning, Miguel boarded a small, crowded boat to Panama City—alone.

For ten long days, Panama became both a refuge and a test of will. He wandered through humid streets, slept in cramped rooms, and searched for passage north. Miguel stepped off the small bus into the humid streets of Panama City, the air thick with salt and diesel. His clothes stuck to his skin, and the weight of his backpack dug into his shoulders. His back ached, and his muscles cried, yet he did not give up. Against the challenging winding path, he found little moments of refuge that kept him going.

He wandered through crowded markets, listening to the chatter of vendors, inhaling the scent of fried plantains and roasting coffee. Nights were long, cramped in small rooms where the ceiling seemed to drip with sweat—and water. Each day brought uncertainty—would he find passage north? Would someone trust him with a ride anymore now that he was on his own?

By the tenth day, he had secured a small boat heading toward Costa Rica. Relief and trepidation mingled in his chest. The past two weeks were just a pre-cap, a small teaser to what was ahead. The journey was only beginning. When he finally secured a boat, his journey picked up speed, as if now he was not the one leading his life. Now the life had taken it upon itself to make him par—through Costa Rica, Honduras, Belize, Guatemala, and Mexico, crossing border after border, each one feeling like both victory and burden.

Crossing into Costa Rica, the air felt cooler, and the jungle greenery stretched in every direction. Miguel's feet ached from walking the cobbled paths, but soon the air cleared, and his ears perked at the birdsongs and his nose sniffed the scent of wet earth after a sudden rainstorm.

At a small roadside café, a man offered him a cup of black coffee and a loaf of bread without asking for payment. Miguel marveled at the generosity, realizing that even in hardship, kindness could find him.

That night, he reflected on how far he had come—the borders he had crossed, the strangers who had helped him, and the courage it took to keep moving forward. He fell asleep reminiscing about Panama behind him and dreaming about the next challenge ahead.

The next morning, his journey took him to Honduras. The place greeted him with winding mountain roads and shanty villages. Miguel felt fatigue pressing down on him. With every step, he carried a reminder of the miles he had already traveled.

At a small inn, he struggled to communicate in broken Spanish with the receptionist. The conversation soon turned into a heated banter. Misunderstandings caused tension, and Miguel could feel all the fatigue turning into an outburst. Yet, he persisted. He pressed his palms together and took deep breaths for half a minute. Later, he realized that the small moment taught him patience along the way.

One night, as he walked through the dimly lit, rocky streets of the village, he thought of his family, of Ecuador, and of the promise he had made to his mother.

He realized that strength wasn't just about moving forward physically—it was about enduring fear, doubt, and uncertainty without giving in. More than physical, it was about how mentally strong and emotionally ready you are when you step out on a path of conviction.

The Caribbean air welcomed him as he crossed into Belize. The narrow and rocky lands of Honduras transitioned into palms swaying in the breeze and the turquoise water of the Caribbean Sea. The salty breeze called to him from a distance. Miguel paused to breathe, savoring the change of scenery.

He met a fisherman who offered him a ride on his boat to the next town. Without wanting to miss the opportunity, he hopped, and both of them shared stories of life along the coast. Miguel listened to the fisherman intently and absorbed the small lessons in generosity and perspective. He learned that many travelers like him come to this coast often, and the fisherman has helped many reach nearer to their destinations. For the first time in days, he felt a spark of hope—the dream of reaching New York felt closer.

That evening, as he slept beneath the open sky on the wobbling boat, he allowed himself a rare smile. The journey was arduous, but he was still standing.

Entering Guatemala, Miguel was struck by the scenery changing from the ebbing waters to the towering mountains and mist that rolled through the valleys. The border crossings tested his nerves; officials asked questions, scrutinized papers, and moved at a frustratingly slow pace.

In a charming little town, he shared a meal with some lovely people who embraced him like family rather than a stranger. Their genuine welcome of him made him feel at home, reminding him of the family he left behind and the dreams that inspire him to keep going.

Every mile brought fear and excitement, mingling into a strange cocktail that kept him alert, alive, and determined. The journey was not easy. Sleeping under trees to escape the rain, bus signs, and sometimes even on the cold, hard ground and left without personal comforts, he realized that courage was not a single act but the sum of small, persistent decisions to keep going.

Finally, after weeks of walking, rowing, and trekking, Miguel crossed into Mexico. Cities buzzed with life; markets overflowed with colors, scents, and sounds. He marveled at the vibrancy and diversity, at the hustle and bustle of each street, and saw every big and small town as part of his adventure.

The next stop after Mexico was his final dream—America, the land where his mother lived, and his dreams dwelt.

As he boarded a bus toward the U.S. border, he whispered a promise to himself: no matter the struggles, no matter the uncertainty, he would arrive. And with that, he settled into his seat, heart racing, ready for the final leg of his odyssey.

On his way to San Antonio, he closed his eyes out of tiredness. The changing scenery and the thought that his journey was now about to end reminded him of the long, winding path he had crossed. He remembered the countless strangers—some kind, others indifferent. A smile broke upon his lips as he thought about that man in Guatemala who shared stories of his own lost family; the young woman in Mexico who taught him the word "hope" in English. With every encounter, Miguel realized that even in a world that often seemed vast and unwelcoming, human connection made it bearable.

At last, after what felt like a lifetime, Miguel stepped onto American soil—San Antonio, Texas—exhausted, exhilarated, and unsure of what came next. From there, he boarded a long, rumbling bus that carried him halfway across the country to Manhattan, New York.

When the doors opened, the city roared to life around him—horns blaring, engines humming, voices shouting in languages he didn't yet understand. How would he find his mother in this big, crowded city with so many faces all swarming around him?

His gloved hands reached into the front pocket of his worn-out jeans, and from among the forgotten bills, he brought out that one thing he would never dare forget—the address of his mother in New York.

He had copied it from the letters that she wrote him, and thankfully, from the first letter to the last that she sent a while ago, the address had not changed.

Motivation piqued in his blood, and adrenaline rushed as he asked people around where he could find his mother's street. Sweating and breathless in the winter air, he walked miles and miles before he finally stepped on the street mentioned in the streets. He recognized it from the pictures she would seldom post along with the letters.

He was here. He was finally here. Now he just had to look out for her home.

And then, suddenly, like a flash, through the crowd, he saw her.

His mother.

María stood on the platform, eyes glistening, holding a small bouquet of flowers. For a moment, time stilled. Miguel's chest tightened, and before he knew it, he was running toward her. His feet forgot all the soreness from the journey as his body collided with his mother's. The two embraced tightly, years of separation melting away in an instant.

"Mijo, estas aqui," she whispered, tears streaking her cheeks (*You're here*).

"Si, lo hice mami," Miguel said, voice trembling. "Te lo promete" (*I made it, mami. I promised you I would*).

María took him by the hand and led him toward the subway—Miguel's first taste of New York's underground maze. The scent of metal, oil, and roasted chestnuts filled the air. When the train roared past, he flinched, then laughed as his mother squeezed his hand.

Upon stepping back into the daylight, Miguel looked up—and the city unfolded before him: towering skyscrapers, yellow taxis, and the distant shimmer of the Statue of Liberty.

"Qué belleza," Miguel murmured, eyes wide (*What beauty*).

"Todo está muy interesante" (*Everything is very interesting*).

María smiled proudly. "Sí, mijo. Y ahora, este es tu hogar" (*Yes, my son. And now, this is your home*).

For the first time, Miguel believed her. The long road from Ecuador had ended. A new one—full of possibility—was just beginning.

2
The Struggle to Belong

The first few months in New York unfolded like a movie Miguel couldn't quite understand—like a film without subtitles, rushing forward faster than he could follow. Everything was happening so quickly that he felt like a stranger stepping into a new world.

Every morning, the city woke with the same rhythm—the hiss of bus brakes, the echo of subway announcements, and the soft hum of people always in a hurry. Miguel admired it all, though he sometimes felt like a quiet observer watching the world from the outside looking in.

It was strange to feel both grateful and overwhelmed at the same time—like his body had arrived, but parts of his heart were still catching up.

It was surreal. He knew he had made it—legally, safely, and with a clean path toward citizenship. Yet, there was still a distance between him and the life around him, something invisible and unspoken. It wasn't fear or regret—it was more like the sensation of being close to home, but not quite inside it.

New Words, New World

English came slowly, like water dripping from a faucet. At the local community college near their Bronx apartment, he sat among other newcomers—men and women from Puerto Rico, Haiti, Italy, Korea, and beyond. They all shared the same goal: to learn enough to be understood, to belong through language.

His teachers, especially one in particular, were patient and kind.

"Miguel," she said one day as he practiced a sentence, "Tienes buen oído para el ritmo. No te preocupes por el acento; es parte de ti" (*You have a good ear for rhythm. Don't worry about the accent; it's part of who you are*).

Miguel smiled shyly and said, "Lo intento, señora. Inglés… es como un rompecabezas; aún no conozco las cartas" (*I try, señora. English… is like a puzzle; I don't know the cards yet*).

The class laughed softly, and Miguel joined in, realizing that laughter was its own kind of language.

Every week, he picked a new word to master: *train*, *thank you*, *tomorrow*. He wrote them on scraps of paper and taped them to the wall above his bed. Maria would peek into his room at night, smiling to herself when she saw the growing collection.

"Vas a mejorar, mijo," she said one evening as they ate dinner. "Estas aprendado rapido" (*You will get better, mijo. You're learning fast*).

Miguel looked at her and nodded. "Simplemente no quiero sonar… tonto" (*I just don't want to sound… foolish*).

"Tonto? Los tontos son las personas que nunca lo intentan," she laughed (*Foolish? The foolish ones are the people who never try*).

By late 1975, Miguel had found steady work helping at a local restaurant in Manhattan. The days were long—chopping vegetables, carrying boxes, cleaning floors—but there was pride in each task. For the first time since arriving, he felt useful—as if the city had finally found a small place for him. The restaurant thrived, drawing a steady stream of hungry patrons each day, and before long, the kitchen came to feel like a second home. The cooks joked, argued, and shared stories about their own journeys.

"Ecuador, eh?" one of them, Luigi, said while stirring a pot of soup. "You people make good ceviche. Maybe one day you cook for us."

Miguel grinned. "Maybe tomorrow."

He came home smelling of onions and garlic, his clothes dusted with flour, his hands sore but steady. At night, he and his mother would sit by the window, listening to the distant honk of taxis. Sometimes they talked about Ecuador—the fruit markets, the music, the soft rain that fell in Guayaquil. Other times, they simply sat in silence, content just to share the same space again; happy that they were together again. In those quiet moments, Miguel felt something he hadn't felt in years—peace that didn't demand anything of him.

Belonging in Pieces

Winter arrived—Miguel's first. Snow fell like something out of a dream, soft and quiet, covering the streets in white. He was not surprised that the cold did not affect him much. It just made his breath visible. He had never owned a heavy coat before, and his mother's laughter filled the apartment as she wrapped a thick scarf around his neck.

"¡No salgas sin esto, que te congelarás!" she called out to him (*Don't go out there without this, or you'll freeze*).

"Mami," he said, half-laughing, "¡No esta frio!" (*Mom, it's not cold*).

He learned to walk carefully on icy sidewalks, to drink hot chocolate after long days, to appreciate the strange beauty of New York blanketed in snow. The city that had once seemed enormous and foreign now felt… welcoming, in its own way.

At church on Sundays with his mother, Miguel met other Ecuadorians who had also come to the States in search of a better life. They traded recipes, news, and family stories. It warmed him to hear familiar accents and to share meals that tasted like home.

And yet, there were nights when he felt caught between two worlds—the one he left behind and the one he was building. He would sometimes stand on the fire escape, watching the lights of Manhattan in the distance, thinking of Guido and wondering what might have happened if they had continued the journey together.

"¿Crees que le gustaría estar aquí?" (*Would he like it here*) Miguel once asked his mother.

Maria thought for a moment. "Quizás. Pero no todos tienen el mismo corazón" (*Maybe. But not everyone's heart beats for the same place*).

Her words lingered with him, soft but sharp—a reminder that some destinies split quietly, long before people do.

A New Kind of Home

By the mid-1980s, Miguel's English had slightly improved, and with it came new opportunities. He began working as a taxi driver, navigating the endless web of streets and learning the rhythms of the city in a way no map could teach. His passengers came from everywhere—businessmen, tourists, students—and every day was a new story. Some rides were loud and chaotic, others quiet and contemplative, but each one taught him something about the heartbeat of the city he was slowly claiming as his own.

He loved the quiet moments most: driving across the Queensboro Bridge at sunset, the skyline glowing gold, the air filled with possibility.

One evening, a passenger asked, "You from here?"

Miguel hesitated, then smiled and said, "Now I am."

It wasn't a lie; New York was now his home.

It was a simple answer, but it carried the weight of his journey. Miguel knew one thing with certainty: he had arrived exactly where he was meant to be.

3
Through A Daughter's Eyes

Growing up, my father often told me that America was the land where dreams could come true—a place of possibility, where even the smallest effort could lead to something meaningful. He never once regretted leaving Ecuador; if anything, he sometimes wondered what might have happened if he had taken that leap even sooner.

He would often sit at the kitchen table, a cup of tea warming his hands, and repeat softly, almost like a prayer: "Este país tiene oportunidades si trabajas duro" (*This country has opportunities if you work hard*).

I used to watch him speak about it with such conviction, as though the air itself carried hope. His eyes always glimmered with that same spark—the one that had carried him across oceans and borders to begin a new life.

My father's philosophy was simple but profound: follow your dreams, and never let fear win. He would look at me and say, "Tienes que ser más fuerte que el miedo, porque la mente es muy poderosa y tú tienes que ser fuerte" (*You have to be stronger than fear, because the mind is powerful, and you must be strong*).

I guess at times, I didn't always understand what he meant. To me, fear felt enormous—an invisible wall that blocked my every step. It seemed easy for him to say, easy for someone who had already proven his courage by traveling alone across countries at nineteen, who had built a life out of sheer willpower.

I often saw him as unshakable: the man who could walk into a room and greet everyone as if he had known them his whole life, who carried himself with confidence and humor, who found positivity in even the smallest things—a sunny day, a stranger's smile, a good meal. The complete opposite of me, or so I believed. But courage rarely looks the way we imagine it. It isn't always loud or fearless. Sometimes it's carried quietly, tucked beneath the routines of everyday life—behind a smile, behind tired eyes, behind a man who refuses to let hardship harden him.

The older I became, the more I realized that we were not so different. Beneath his confidence was a quiet determination that came from struggle—the kind that doesn't fade, only softens over time. I began to understand that courage is not loud; sometimes it looks like someone who keeps going even when no one is watching.

My father and I were mirrors of one another. We both carried the same yearning—to belong, to feel understood, to create something meaningful with our lives. We both had our doubts and insecurities, though we showed them differently. He disguised his with laughter; I hid mine in silence. Yet, in our own ways, we both leaned on faith. He trusted in God's timing, and I trusted in the lessons he left me.

One evening, I remember asking him, "Papi, weren't you ever scared when you left Ecuador?"

He smiled softly, staring at the steam rising from his cup. "Por supesto, tenía miedo, muchoisimo miedo," he said (*Of course, I was scared—very scared*).

"But I was more scared of never trying. If I stayed, I would always wonder what if? Sometimes, hija, the risk is not leaving—it's staying where you are."

That conversation has stayed with me for years. It was in that moment that I realized courage doesn't mean you're fearless—it means you move forward with fear, not against it. For years, it sat quietly in the back of my mind until the moment I truly understood what he meant.

It happened when I traveled to Ecuador for the first time as a teenager. I remember stepping off the plane, the humid air wrapping around me, the sound of vendors calling outside, the streets alive with color and movement. I had heard about Ecuador all my life, but being there—seeing it through my own eyes—changed something in me.

I met family I had only seen in pictures: cousins, aunts, uncles, and grandparents. Their warmth was immediate. Their smiles felt familiar. And yet, beneath their joy, I could see the weight of their struggles. I saw how hard they worked, how much they dreamed, how the opportunities my father had found in America were still just that—dreams—for many of them.

Work was steady for some and unpredictable for others, and life was different for people. But what struck me most wasn't poverty—it was resilience. My family never complained. They laughed, they cooked together, they prayed. They found joy in simple things: a shared meal, a song on the radio, a child's laughter echoing in the courtyard.

Watching them, I understood my father's longing—not just for opportunity, but for the chance to honor the people who had raised him, to lift them through the life he was building abroad.

That visit changed me. For the first time, I understood what my father had left behind—not just a place, but people. People he loved deeply. He had left so that his family could have more, not because he didn't love Ecuador, but because he dreamed of giving something greater back to it.

When I returned home to New York, I noticed everything differently. The tall buildings, the fast trains, even the steady hum of the city—all of it carried new meaning. I understood now why my father worked so hard, why he never let fear or fatigue stop him. He wasn't just building a life for himself; he was carrying his entire family's hopes on his shoulders.

I realized that for many immigrants like my father, success isn't measured by what you personally gain—but by what you can give to others.

My father always said, "If one of us succeeds, we all succeed."

That was his definition of the American dream: not wealth, but legacy.

When my father asked me to write this book, I didn't hesitate. I knew I had to tell his story—not just the story of an immigrant chasing a dream, a possibility, but of a man whose courage became the foundation for the generations after him. He wanted me to capture not only his journey but the essence of what it meant: faith, perseverance, love, and the belief that even the simplest beginnings can lead to something extraordinary.

As I write these words, I think of my grandmother, Maria, the woman who greeted him when he first arrived in New York. I imagine her taking his hand in that bustling subway station, guiding him through the noise and the lights of a city that never seemed to sleep. But I also think of the day she arrived in the country completely alone—what must have gone through her mind, what fears she held quietly, what hopes kept her moving forward.

I think of my other grandmother, who also immigrated from Ecuador, leaving my mother, grandfather, and uncles behind. And I think of my mother, whose own story of migration intertwines with each of theirs in ways neither could have imagined.

Writing this book is my way of honoring them—every sacrifice, every tear, every prayer whispered for a better life. My family's story is not one of struggle alone, but of grace and faith.

My father always believed that everything in life came with a lesson.

"La vida te enseña si estás dispuesto a escuchar," he would remind me (*Life teaches you if you are willing to listen*).

For him, every challenge—learning English, working long hours, being far from home—was another way to grow stronger, to learn gratitude, to trust that God would never close one door without opening another. And somewhere along the way, I realized his lessons had quietly become my compass, guiding me through my own fears, reminding me that courage can be inherited just like stories.

Maybe that's what this story truly is—not just a story about immigration, but about transformation. About finding a sense of home not only in a new land but within yourself.

I sometimes imagine what my father must have felt when he first saw the New York skyline, when the Statue of Liberty appeared in view, when the hum of the city wrapped around him like a promise. It's hard not to get emotional thinking about it—how one decision to leave behind everything familiar led to a life that would one day make my story possible.

When I was younger, I didn't fully understand what his journey meant. Now, as an adult, I see it clearly: his courage gave me choices. His sacrifices built the foundation that allows me to dream freely, to write, to tell stories, to express the same hope he carried in his heart.

So, this book—this story—is more than a chronicle of events. It's a letter of admiration. To my father, to my family, and to every person who has ever left home searching for something greater. Because home, I've learned, is not always where you begin. Sometimes, it's what you build along the way—through faith, love, and the quiet courage to begin again.

4
A Life of Independence

By the early 1980s, Miguel had begun to feel at home in New York. The city, once dizzying and overwhelming, now moved in rhythms he could understand. He knew the subway lines, the streets, the corners where the best coffee and the cheapest hot dogs could be found. Every hum, honk, and hurried step was no longer foreign—it was familiar.

He often found himself smiling at the small details he once overlooked—the way steam rose from street grates in the winter, the morning rush of people balancing coffee cups and briefcases, the elderly men playing dominoes outside the corner store. These scenes, once overwhelming, had become the backdrop of his new life.

For a time, he continued living with his mother, Maria, in their modest apartment in the Bronx. Their days were comfortable yet full. Miguel helped with chores, cooked meals when she came home from work, and spent evenings catching up on English lessons or reading books borrowed from the community library. Life had its routine, but it was a routine Miguel cherished. Living with his mother kept him grounded and reminded him of the sacrifices his family had made, and of the love that had followed him across the world.

There was a comfort in those quiet evenings. Maria humming while washing dishes, the gentle clink of cutlery, the sound of Spanish radio playing boleros in the background—these small rituals made their little apartment feel warm and safe, a piece of Ecuador tucked inside the Bronx.

Still, Miguel's spirit of independence could not be contained. While he was grateful to live with Maria, he began to dream of a life on his own—a space that was entirely his. One year, after much careful saving, he moved into a small apartment in the same building. It was a modest space, just enough for a bed, a small kitchen, and a living area, but to Miguel, it felt like freedom.

He remembered unlocking the door for the first time and standing in the center of the empty room, listening to its silence. It was the first silence that belonged entirely to him.

He delighted in the little things: arranging his books just so, cooking his favorite meals whenever he wished, choosing the music that played through the apartment. No one was around to judge his choices or to question his pace. For the first time, he felt fully responsible for himself—and he relished it.

Even with his new independence, Miguel's life was never idle. He worked various jobs—sometimes as a home health aide, sometimes in construction, other times cooking or driving a taxi. Each job came with its own rhythm. Construction taught him patience; cooking taught him precision; taxi driving taught him to read people—their moods, their silences, their stories. Miguel took pride not just in earning money, but in discovering who he could become. He enjoyed the variety, the movement, and the sense that he was constantly learning.

Miguel also made time to build friendships. He often met fellow immigrants at community centers, cafés, and neighborhood gatherings. Their conversations ranged from the practical—tips for taxes, how to navigate the city—to the philosophical—dreams, fears, and memories of home. Evenings, after a long day at work, were spent gathering at a corner café, sharing stories in Spanish and English, their words weaving a bridge between the lives they had left behind and the lives they were creating. Over time, these connections became a network of support, laughter, and shared experience, a community of his own.

And then there were his travels. Even settled in New York, Miguel could not stay in one place for too long. His love for the world and curiosity about people and places remained insatiable. He returned to Europe frequently, exploring cities and countrysides, discovering new cultures, and reconnecting with familiar ones. Italy remained a favorite—he found a rhythm there, a sense of belonging in its streets, cafés, and piazzas. Each journey offered lessons: patience in waiting for trains, humility in language barriers, and joy in the generosity of strangers.

He often said that travel reminded him that the world was bigger than his struggles. He collected moments as triklets: a shared meal, friendly gestures, a breathtaking view.

Miguel's life as a single bachelor was simple yet rich. He met friends from every corner of the city, from co-workers to fellow travelers he met abroad. Dinners, tennis games, weekend excursions to nearby beaches, scuba diving adventures in the Caribbean—each moment filled his days with joy and experience. Though he had no family of his own at the time, his world was full of connection, adventure, and opportunity.

And throughout all of this, Miguel never lost his grounding. All that shine of the new world never distracted him from gratitude—for his mother, for his home, for the life he had built with his own two hands.

Living independently also allowed him to focus on his own growth. He continued learning, both formally and informally, and embraced each new experience as a way to understand the world and himself. He spent weekends at museums, galleries, and local theaters, not only for enjoyment but also as inspiration. He kept journals of thoughts, sketches, and reflections on what he observed, capturing the richness of city life and the diversity of human experience. Journals that later became treasures, housing a wealth of knowledge that helped in the making of this book.

There were days when independence brought challenges for Miguel. There were nights when loneliness crept in, when the city's noise seemed too loud and the streets too vast.

On those nights, he would call his mother; her familiar voice coming from the speaker would ground him like magic.

"Todo va a estar bien, mijo," she'd say (*Everything is going to be okay, my son*).

And somehow, it always was.

And so, Miguel had learned resilience. He reminded himself of the journey from Ecuador, of the courage it took to leave home, and of the life he had been building. Every obstacle became a lesson, every hardship a reminder that freedom came with responsibility.

New York remained his anchor. He returned each time from travels with a deeper appreciation for the life he had built: the apartment he could call his own, the jobs that supported him, the mother who cheered him on, and the friendships that enriched his days. Miguel thrived not only because of his accomplishments but because of the freedom to shape his own life and the courage to embrace it fully.

He understood that independence wasn't about having everything—it was about being grateful for what he had, and trusting himself to create what he didn't.

As a young man living alone, he understood that independence was not just about space or finances—it was about trust: trusting himself, trusting his instincts, and trusting that the foundation he had built in a new country could support him as he explored the world. He learned to celebrate small victories: cooking a perfect meal, fixing a broken appliance, or navigating a day in the city without a hitch. These moments, seemingly minor, reinforced his confidence and sense of agency.

And in those early years of independence, he had to grip on to his belief that everything would work out in the end. In those moments, he realized that self-reliance is a skill that needs to be reinforced again and again. It is something that grows the more you showcase it, and it grows stronger each time life presents a challenge.

For Miguel, this period of his life was a balance of stability and adventure—a rare combination that allowed him to enjoy the fruits of his labor while continuing to grow, learn, and explore. It was the life of a man who had made it to a new land, who had found home, and who was now ready to define his own path—a path full of possibility, freedom, and quiet joy.

And in his quiet moments, gazing out at the Bronx skyline, he reflected on a deeper truth: independence was not a destination but a process, a daily commitment to oneself, to curiosity, and to the courage to live fully. He realized that the life he built was not just for him—it was an inspiration, a testament to anyone willing to step into the unknown and claim their own place in the world.

A Daughter's Reflection

Looking back, I realize how much my father's independence shaped not only his life but mine. As I watched him navigate the city on his own, meet new people, and take chances—from jobs to travels—I began to understand what courage and self-reliance truly meant. Independence was not about being alone; it was about creating a life with intention, about making choices that reflected his values, and about embracing responsibility for every decision.

To me, he always seemed so sure of himself, but I now understand that his confidence was earned—built slowly through years of trial, error, heartbreak, discovery, and hope.

Even as a young child, I noticed the rhythm of his life. The way he returned from work with stories of the city and people he met, the way he planned trips to Europe or Caribbean islands, and the way he balanced work with learning and curiosity—all of it left a mark on me. I began to see that life could be approached with both discipline and wonder, that work and joy were not opposing forces but partners in a full life.

I remember asking him once why he traveled so often, and he smiled, eyes twinkling. "Porque quiero que veas el mundo, hija," he said (*Because I want you to see the world, daughter*).

Even then, I understood that his independence was never selfish. It was about exploration, growth, and sharing the lessons of life with those he loved. He wanted me to understand that a full life required both roots and wings—and he hoped to give me both.

Through his example, I learned that freedom comes with responsibility. It is not just about having choices, but about honoring them, working for them, and using them to build something meaningful. Independence is also about resilience—about continuing forward, even when life is uncertain, and having faith that every step, every small decision, contributes to a life worth living. That fear doesn't disappear; it just becomes smaller when you move away.

And now, years later, I see that the values Miguel built into his independent life are part of my own foundation. His courage, curiosity, and persistence guide my choices. His dedication to learning, his openness to people, and his joy in simple moments remind me that independence is both a personal gift and a family legacy. I know that his journey shaped the woman I have become, someone who believes in possibilities because he lived it first.

In witnessing his life, I learned that independence is not just about living alone or being self-sufficient. It is about creating a space where dreams can flourish, where joy is intentional, and where life is lived fully, with curiosity and courage. It is a lesson I carry with me every day—a quiet, enduring reflection of the man my father is, and the life he built with heart and determination.

5
Family and Legacy

As Miguel settled into life in New York, he began to build a family of his own. His journey in love and parenthood was not without its challenges, but it reflected the life he had chosen—one defined by courage, resilience, and an unwavering sense of hope. He never pretended to have all the answers. What he did have was heart—an instinct to keep showing up, even when life felt uncertain or complicated.

In his early years in America, Miguel married briefly and welcomed his first son. It was a time when he was still learning how to balance dreams with duty—a young man far from home, determined to build something solid on uncertain ground. Though that chapter of his life was short, it marked the beginning of his journey as a father and a provider in a country that was still new to him.

He took pride in small victories: steady work, a paycheck earned honestly, the roof over his head. Miguel may not have spoken much about his struggles, but those who knew him could see the weight of responsibility he carried—not as a burden, but as a measure of love. To him, providing was not just about money—it was about presence, intention, and the quiet promise that he would always try his best, even when circumstances were imperfect.

Later, he had another son from a different relationship, continuing to expand his family while navigating the complexities of life and fatherhood. Each of his children represented a part of his story—his sacrifices, his lessons, his hopes for a better future.

By the time Miguel met my mother, he was older, wiser, and more grounded in the man he had become. Together, they created a home filled with warmth, laughter, and faith. Ours was not a house of luxury, but of love—a place where the scent of home-cooked meals filled the kitchen, and the sound of music from both Ecuador and America blended in the background.

Miguel carried the traditions of his homeland into this new chapter of his life. He spoke Spanish around the house, reminded us to be proud of where we came from, and told stories of his childhood in Ecuador—the long walks to school, the laughter of friends, the dreams that once seemed impossible. My mother matched his strength with tenderness, creating balance in our home. Together, they taught me that family is not only built through blood, but through commitment, faith, and understanding.

Holidays were a blend of cultures. Ecuadorian dishes next to American ones, Spanish prayers before meals, and the warmth of a family gathered in one small Bronx apartment. Those moments taught me that identity could be woven from many threads.

Though some parts of his personal life remain private, one truth stands above all: Miguel made a life here. He built it with his own two hands—not from privilege or ease, but from perseverance. He worked long hours, often leaving before sunrise and returning after dark, yet he never failed to smile when he walked through the door. He believed in showing rather than telling—teaching us through his actions that success is not about what you have, but how you earn it.

Even on the hardest days, he tried to bring light into the home—a small joke, a warm hug, or a reminder that "mañana será mejor" (*tomorrow will be better*). For him, optimism was a form of faith.

He taught his children to dream beyond what they saw in front of them.

"No tengas miedo de intentar," he would say (*Don't be afraid to try*).

To him, fear was not something to avoid but something to confront. Every risk he took, leaving home, starting over, building anew, had been guided by that same belief. He often told us that courage wasn't loud; sometimes it sounded like a quiet prayer, or the steady footsteps of someone who keeps going even when tired.

As his daughter, I often think about how his story, though quiet and humble, became the foundation of ours. He didn't need to leave behind great wealth or fame; what he left behind was far greater—a legacy of courage, compassion, and determination.

When I look at the life he created—the family that now spans generations, the stories that bind us together—I see a man who never stopped believing that his choices mattered. He may have come to this country with little more than a dream, but what he built was a testament to what dreams, when pursued with heart and conviction, can become.

Even now, when our family gathers, his influence fills the room—in our laughter, in our values, in the way we hold on to one another. His legacy is not only in the family he raised, but in the lessons that continue to echo through us—that success is earned, that love endures, and that no matter where life takes us, we must always carry pride in where we began. Through him, we learned to honor our roots along with embracing our future, a balance that shaped every generation after him.

Miguel's life was proof that even the simplest story—one without fanfare or fame—can hold extraordinary meaning. Because in his journey, there is a universal truth: that to build a life of love, family, and purpose is the greatest success of all. And perhaps the greatest lesson of all was this: that a meaningful life is not measured in recognition, but in the quiet impact one person leaves on the hearts of many.

A Daughter's Reflection

As I've grown older, I've come to realize how deeply my father's values have shaped me. I often think back to his quiet strength—how he worked hard without complaint, how he found joy in the smallest things, and how he never stopped believing in the promise of a better tomorrow. His lessons weren't given in long speeches, but through the way he lived.

There are moments when I find myself repeating his words: "Tienes que ser más fuerte que el miedo" (*You have to be stronger than fear*).

Those words have carried me through challenges I never thought I could face. They remind me that the same courage that brought him across continents lives within me, too. Whenever I doubt myself, I hear his voice—calm, steady, certain—reminding me that fear is merely a doorway, not a wall.

Writing this book has been my way of saying thank you for the sacrifices, for the laughter, and for the love that built the foundation of who I am today. My father's story may not be filled with hardship or tragedy, but it shines in its own quiet strength. It's a story of perseverance, faith, and family—and it continues to inspire me every single day.

In honoring his story, I am honoring the many who walked similar paths, people whose names may never appear in books, but whose lives shaped generations with quiet courage.

6
Becoming a Father, Building a Future

Once Miguel becomes a father, the abstract ideas of responsibility and legacy take on a vivid, immediate meaning. The tiny hands of his children, the soft cries in the night, the quiet moments of worry and joy—all of it affirms the life he has chosen. In these moments, Miguel knows with certainty that he is exactly where he is meant to be. For him, the lullabies and small hands in the dark: the weight of a sleeping child on his chest, the tiny fingers that curl around his thumb, the hush of the apartment after a long day. Those quiet repetitions, the nightly songs, the whispered stories, the slow, steady breathing, become the proof of everything he's building.

Fatherhood changes him in ways that are subtle but profound. He moves through the city differently now, noticing the world not only for himself but for those who depend on him. Every paycheck, every decision, and even the sacrifices of sleep or comfort carry a new weight—one rooted in love and purpose rather than fear or necessity. He has come to New York not just to survive, but to thrive in ways that can nurture the next generation.

Even amidst the exhaustion, Miguel finds joy in teaching. He shows his children the value of hard work, not through words alone, but by example. Early mornings in the kitchen, evenings filled with homework and quiet talks, weekends exploring the city or simply walking through local parks—every ordinary moment becomes a lesson in perseverance, curiosity, and integrity.

"Cada día cuenta," he says (*Every day counts*).

As the years pass, Miguel's vision for his children becomes clearer. He wants them to have opportunities he could only dream of as a boy in Guayaquil. He wants them to see the world, to learn its languages and rhythms, to meet its people, and to carry forward the values that have guided him: courage, resilience, and a quiet, steady determination.

Travel becomes a way for Miguel to teach these lessons. Even before long trips are feasible, he talks to them about the places he has seen, cities that hum with life, mountains, and rivers that shape the lands he visits. When his children are old enough, he takes them on their first journeys beyond the city—short trips at first, then longer ones—showing them not only the world but how to navigate it with curiosity, patience, and respect.

On those trips, he watches them react, the wide eyes at a mountain's scale, the impatient laughter on a ferry, the shy attempts at a new phrase, and feels a quiet, almost private pride. It isn't the postcard moments that matter most; it's the small victories: a child asking for directions, trying a new food, or sharing a laugh with a stranger. Those scenes become the stitches of a life Miguel knows will hold.

Through fatherhood, Miguel also reflects on the weight of past choices. Previous hardships and sacrifices no longer feel like burdens; they are lessons that now shape the path he walks with his children. Every decision, every risk he has taken to leave Ecuador, every lonely night in a new country—all of it has led to this moment, this family, this life.

Family becomes not just a refuge but a compass. Laughter around the dinner table, shared meals, occasional arguments, and celebrations of milestones—each thread weaves a tapestry of love and learning. Miguel's children grow up with an understanding that life is not always easy, but it can be full of purpose, joy, and meaning if lived with intention.

Miguel understands the importance of balance. Hard work is vital, but so is presence. Even when long hours pull him away, he makes sure his children know they are his priority. From teaching them Spanish and sharing stories of Ecuador to encouraging them to pursue their passions, he instills pride in both their heritage and their potential. Looking at his life now, Miguel sees that fatherhood is the true measure of success. It is not fame, wealth, or accolades, but the love, guidance, and values he passes on. Each small moment, each choice guided by integrity and care, contributes to a legacy that continues to grow—in his children, in their choices, and in the life they build together.

Fatherhood teaches Miguel that legacy is built in quiet, steady acts of love, discipline, and guidance—in teaching children to dream, to work, and to carry themselves with pride. His life as a father reflects the essence of his journey: courage paired with compassion, ambition balanced by care, and a commitment to shaping a future brighter than the past. And as his children grow, Miguel's lessons continue to guide them— in the way they approach life, in how they value family, and in how they carry his example forward. He is living proof that ordinary beginnings, met with determination, faith, and courage, can create a life full of meaning and possibility.

7
Rediscovering Dreams Through Young Eyes

Miguel eventually found steady employment as a school bus driver, a job that brought more adventures than he ever expected.

Winter Magic

One December, the bus took the children past the Rockefeller Center Christmas tree. The air was crisp, and the lights reflected in the children's wide eyes. Miguel watched as a little boy pressed his hands against the window, marveling at the ice skaters below. He remembered the first time he had seen the tree as a child—bundled against the cold, shivering with excitement, utterly captivated.

That winter, he shared stories of snow in Central Park, of the first hot chocolate he had ever tasted, and the children listened as if discovering the city for the first time themselves. Miguel smiled at their wonder, realizing that these moments were more than field trips; they were gateways to curiosity. He watched a little girl tug at her friend's sleeve, pointing to a street performer juggling lights.

"Look!" she whispered. "It's like magic!"

Sometimes, as he watched the kids chatter and press their faces to the windows, Miguel felt a quiet warmth spread through him—the kind that comes not from nostalgia, but from witnessing wonder in real time. It reminded him that life always offers a second chance to feel amazed, no matter how many winters have passed. In that winter glow, he reflected: the city had not only given him opportunities, it had also taught him the value of seeing life through others' eyes. Every snowflake, every glowing ornament, every skater spinning on ice was a reminder that magic exists when we take the time to notice.

Spring Adventures

During spring, the students visited the Museum of Modern Art. Miguel had arranged for the field trip, eager to show them the paintings and sculptures that had inspired him as a young man. He watched as a group of children clustered around a bright, abstract painting, debating what the shapes could mean.

"It's like a dream!" one girl exclaimed.

Miguel smiled, thinking how, years ago, he had stood before the same painting, unsure what he was seeing but feeling his imagination ignite. He remembered feeling both lost and exhilarated, wondering if he would ever understand art, and realizing that the joy was in the trying, the exploring, the imagining.

He walked the aisles with them, encouraging questions, offering bits of history, and witnessing curiosity flare in young eyes.

"Why is that sculpture twisting like that?" a boy asked, pointing to a metallic figure.

Miguel explained, "The artist wanted to show movement—how even metal can seem alive if you look closely."

He watched the boy nod thoughtfully, and in that moment, Miguel felt a profound connection between his past and the present: that same spark of wonder that had fueled his youth was now alive in another generation.

So as the children moved from one gallery to another, Miguel noticed how differently each child responded—some wide-eyed, some skeptical, some quietly absorbing it all. Their reactions reminded him that imagination blooms in its own time, and that part of guiding children is simply creating space for them to discover themselves.

Summer Surprises

One summer, the children were scheduled to see a Broadway rehearsal, a special treat Miguel had coordinated through the school. The kids whispered in anticipation as the performers danced across the stage, and Miguel could hear their gasps and laughter.

"I've never seen anything like this!" a student shouted.

Miguel remembered that awe from his first show, when he had felt the thrill of lights, music, and movement for the very first time.

Seeing them now, he realized that the magic of discovery was timeless—something that could be shared and relived, over and over again, in each new generation. He noticed one student lingering after the performance, eyes wide as he traced every detail with fascination.

Miguel crouched beside him and whispered, "That feeling? Never forget it. Let it take you places." The boy nodded, promising to hold the memory close.

Walking back toward the bus, Miguel noticed how the kids' conversations buzzed with new dreams— some wanted to dance onstage, others wanted to learn instruments, and one shy girl whispered that she wanted to draw costumes someday. Hearing their hopes made Miguel think about how inspiration often arrives quietly, like a seed planted during an ordinary afternoon.

Miguel also began to see the deeper meaning in his work: that his role was not just to drive the bus or supervise trips, but to cultivate curiosity and wonder. He started to intentionally tell stories, recall his own first experiences, and invite the children to see themselves in new possibilities. Every awe-filled reaction was a lesson—not just for them, but for him too.

Everyday Wonders

Even in ordinary moments, Miguel noticed small delights—a street musician strumming a guitar, children discovering a painted mural on a neighborhood wall, or the first snowflake of winter landing on a student's sleeve. Each encounter became a teaching moment, a memory embedded into both his heart and theirs.

Sometimes, after long days, he would reflect quietly on the bus. Watching children lean forward, eyes wide, hands pressed against the windows, he thought about how life's beauty often reveals itself in fleeting moments. It wasn't only museums or Broadway; it was the ordinary, unnoticed details—the architecture of a brownstone, the laughter of friends, the rhythm of a city waking up. Through these glimpses, Miguel learned that wonder was everywhere if you only paused to notice it.

Through these seasons, Miguel realized that life's greatest joy was not in achieving dreams for himself alone, but in nurturing wonder in others. Every laugh, gasp, and moment of awe reinforced the truth he had carried since Ecuador: curiosity is a gift, and sharing it is a responsibility. He thought of his own childhood, the first glimpses of a city beyond his small neighborhood, the inspiration and hope that those early experiences had sown in him. Now, he could give that gift back—a circle of discovery passed from one generation to the next.

By the time the school year ended, Miguel's heart was full. The bus was more than a vehicle; it was a vessel of inspiration, a moving classroom of possibility. And as he prepared for the next round of children, he reminded himself that the city was vast, the world was full of wonders, and part of life's purpose was helping others to see it. He knew that some of these children would remember these trips for years, perhaps decades, just as he remembered the first time he walked through museums, theaters, and streets that seemed larger than life.

He also reflected on what it meant to connect young eyes to history, art, and culture. For him, it wasn't just about imparting knowledge—it was about cultivating hope, ambition, and imagination. Each child represented a chance to rekindle the dreams he once had, a reminder that wonder and opportunity are evergreen if you allow yourself to see them.

And in the quiet moments, as the bus rolled home and the sun dipped below the skyline, Miguel understood something profound: life's magic is not merely in the places you visit, but in the eyes of those who see them for the first time. To witness that is to rediscover the world anew, to remember why you chase dreams, and to recognize the power of sharing joy, curiosity, and inspiration with those who will carry it forward.

8
A World of Experiences

Even as Miguel built a life in New York and raised a family, his love for travel never faded. The world, with its vast landscapes, cultures, and histories, called to him constantly. Each journey was an opportunity to learn, to meet new people, and to experience life in ways that expanded his understanding of himself and the world around him.

He traveled extensively throughout Europe, visiting France, Italy, Spain, Denmark, Ukraine, and beyond. In Paris, he wandered along the Seine, soaking in the soft light of early morning, marveling at the architecture of Notre-Dame and the Louvre. The aroma of fresh bread and coffee from corner cafés filled the streets, and he found himself exchanging smiles with strangers over shared pastries. A young couple invited him to join their picnic near the Eiffel Tower, and for a few hours, he felt the warmth of connection in a foreign land.

Each city offered a rhythm of life, a history etched in stone and song, and lessons in patience and curiosity. Sometimes, Miguel found himself pausing in quiet corners of these cities—small parks, narrow alleys, riverbanks where locals lingered. In those still moments, he realized how travel reshaped him not through grand monuments, but through glimpses of everyday life.

Italy held a special place in his heart. In Rome, he strolled along cobbled streets, past ancient ruins, feeling the weight of centuries and the vibrancy of daily life. Venice enchanted him with its labyrinth of canals, the gentle lapping of water against gondolas, and the voices of musicians echoing through narrow passageways. Florence taught him to see life in layers of color and shadow, as he marveled at masterpieces in galleries and struck up conversations with local artists. Each trip reminded him that life was an ongoing lesson in wonder, discovery, and human connection.

Miguel also explored Latin America and the Caribbean, visiting relatives, reconnecting with old friends, and meeting new people along the way. In Mexico City, he wandered through bustling markets, inhaling the scent of spices, fresh tortillas, and roasted corn. Music flowed from every corner—mariachi bands in plazas, street performers playing percussion, and singers on street corners whose voices told stories of joy and hardship. In Costa Rica, he hiked through rainforests alive with color, chirping birds, and the occasional howler monkey, feeling both humbled and invigorated by nature's beauty. In Cuba, he danced alongside locals in sun-soaked squares, laughing as he tried to keep up with intricate steps and rhythms, realizing that joy could be shared without words.

What struck him most on these trips was how quickly strangers became companions. Whether sharing a bench in a bustling plaza or standing in line at a food stall, conversations unfolded naturally. People spoke freely about their families, their struggles, and their dreams. Miguel often left these encounters feeling unexpectedly uplifted, reminded that generosity and warmth didn't require familiarity, only willingness.

Through his travels, Miguel met countless people from different walks of life—fellow travelers, local artisans, students, elders with stories to share, and even children whose laughter reminded him of his own youth. A young artist in Florence taught him the patience to look beyond the obvious, to appreciate the details others might overlook. An elderly woman in Seville shared tales of survival and resilience, reminding him that strength comes from enduring hardships with grace. In Ukraine, a fellow traveler became a friend despite the language barrier, proving that curiosity and kindness are universal. Each encounter left a mark on his heart, reinforcing his belief in empathy, openness, and the beauty of connection across cultures.

Even while exploring the world, New York remained his anchor. It was his base, his home, and the city that had given him opportunities he never imagined. Yet each journey reminded him of the freedom he had earned—the ability to live fully, to explore, and to embrace life without hesitation. He returned from each trip with souvenirs, photographs, and stories, but more importantly, he returned with gratitude for the life he had built.

One of Miguel's most cherished experiences was traveling with his children. He wanted them to see the world as he had, to feel the excitement and awe that had inspired him since his youth. Watching their eyes widen in museums, gasp at the grandeur of historical landmarks, or laugh with delight at street performers brought him immense joy. Their wonder mirrored his own first encounters with these marvels in New York and Europe, and he felt proud to share the curiosity and appreciation that had shaped his life.

Sometimes, as he watched them explore a new place—hesitant at first, then bold with excitement—Miguel felt something shift inside him. Seeing the world through their eyes softened the edges of his own responsibilities. It reminded him that despite the challenges of adulthood, joy could still be simple, that these moments could become anchors in their family's story, small but meaningful threads woven into their memories.

Travel for Miguel was more than sightseeing; it was a philosophy, a reflection of how he chose to live. Each trip, each friendship, each discovery taught him lessons in resilience, kindness, and humility. He saw that the world is full of stories waiting to be heard, beauty waiting to be appreciated, and people waiting to be known. These experiences enriched his spirit, informed his values, and inspired the lessons he shared with his children.

Through travel, work, and personal growth, Miguel exemplified a life of balance: rooted in responsibility yet always reaching outward toward the unknown. He celebrated the comfort of home while embracing the wonder of the world. In his stories, in the laughter of his children, and in quiet reflection after each journey, Miguel showed that life is meant to be explored, appreciated, and shared—a life built on courage, curiosity, and the endless pursuit of knowledge and connection.

9
The Power of Dreams

My father's story is not one of tragedy. It is not a tale of unimaginable hardship, nor is it a story filled with horror or despair. Yet, it is a story that deserves to be told—a story that proves that even ordinary challenges, when met with courage and determination, can lead to extraordinary outcomes.

Miguel's journey began with hope. Leaving Ecuador, he stepped into the unknown, unsure of what awaited him, yet certain that America offered possibilities worth pursuing. He faced uncertainty—navigating new countries, learning a new language, and being far from family—but he did so with perseverance and belief in a better future. His life was not perfect, and the road was not always smooth, yet every decision he made built the foundation for the life he would create.

What makes his story remarkable is that it demonstrates the value of ordinary courage. You do not have to face unimaginable danger to have a story worth telling. Sometimes, the power of a dream lies in simply taking steps toward it, even when the path is uncertain or the challenges feel small yet persistent. My father's life is an example of this principle in action.

Although his path was modest, each step required a quiet steadiness—an inner discipline that is easy to overlook. There is a kind of bravery in waking up each day and choosing to begin again, even when progress feels slow or invisible. His story shows that strength often exists not in grand gestures but in the steady commitment to keep moving forward.

He worked multiple jobs to support himself, learning new skills along the way. He took night classes to improve his English, navigated the sprawling streets of New York, and discovered ways to balance responsibility with curiosity. Even traveling alone to countries he had never seen before required confidence and adaptability. These were not heroic feats in the traditional sense, but they were acts of bravery in their own quiet, consistent way.

There were moments when the unfamiliar felt overwhelming—new expectations, new systems, and new cultural rhythms—but Miguel learned to adapt one small challenge at a time. That steady adjustment, that ability to bend without breaking, became one of his greatest strengths. He built a sense of belonging slowly, through effort, patience, and a willingness to learn.

I remember listening to him describe his adventures and thinking about how much courage it took to explore the world without anyone accompanying him. While he cherished the freedom of traveling alone, he also carried the weight of responsibility and the knowledge that each choice he made was shaping his life. From Europe to the Caribbean, from Italy's bustling streets to the serene beaches of the islands, Miguel embraced each experience fully, learning and growing with every step.

Even when the challenges were small—navigating a new city, figuring out bus routes, or starting a new job—he faced them with determination. These ordinary struggles, compounded over time, built the resilience that allowed him to thrive in a foreign land. They were proof that success does not always come from dramatic leaps or extreme circumstances, but from persistence, adaptability, and belief in oneself.

For our family, his story is a source of inspiration. We admire the choices he made, the life he built, and the example he set. Though we did not witness every moment, we see the results: a life of independence, travel, love, and accomplishment. We see the children he raised, the lessons he imparted, and the way he continues to encourage us to dream, take risks, and persevere.

His journey taught us that success is not only measured in fame or fortune. It is measured in growth, in experience, in the ability to create a meaningful life. Miguel's story shows that even without extreme hardship, even without dramatic tragedy, it is possible to achieve dreams—to leave a lasting legacy—simply by taking steady, courageous steps toward a vision you believe in.

I carry this lesson with me every day. His life reminds me that challenges—even ordinary ones—are not obstacles to fear, but opportunities to prove your strength. It reminds me that dreams are possible to achieve when met with faith, dedication, and courage. Miguel's journey, though not long or harrowing in the conventional sense, is powerful precisely because it shows that perseverance, belief in oneself, and a willingness to act can create extraordinary lives from ordinary beginnings.

His story reminds us that meaning is often created in the quiet choices we make—showing up, working hard, staying hopeful, and treating others with respect. These choices, repeated over the years, shape not only the life we build but the example we leave for those who follow.

While this story may be brief, it is full of meaning. It is proof that courage does not always roar; sometimes it whispers quietly, guiding us forward. In the quiet courage of my father's life, I see a life lived fully—a life that inspires, teaches, and reminds us that the possibilities before us are endless when we are willing to step into them.

10
Finding His Place and Becoming an American

After years of building a life in New York—learning the language, working long hours, traveling the world, and raising a family—Miguel reached a milestone he had long dreamed of: becoming an American citizen.

Though we were not there to witness it, and some of us were not yet born, the story of that day has always stayed with us. It is remembered not just as a moment of personal achievement but as a symbol of courage, determination, and perseverance. It is the kind of moment that defines a life quietly, steadily, and profoundly.

Miguel described the courthouse as crowded and alive with anticipation. People of all ages, backgrounds, and languages sat together, each carrying a story of leaving something behind, each hoping to claim a new beginning. Some came with families, others alone; some looked anxious, others joyful. Miguel, sitting among them, felt a mix of pride, humility, and gratitude. Every moment of struggle that brought him to that hall—the long hours, the uncertainty, the loneliness of leaving home—seemed to crystallize in that single, powerful ceremony.

As he waited, Miguel felt the atmosphere around him deepen—an unspoken understanding shared among strangers who had walked their own winding paths to reach that room. There was a softness in the way people looked at one another, as if acknowledging the weight of each journey without needing details. In that quiet exchange, Miguel sensed a collective hope, a feeling that they were stepping into something larger than themselves.

Reciting the oath, Miguel understood that citizenship was more than a legal formality. It was a statement of possibility, a tangible acknowledgment of the journey he had undertaken. It was proof that a young man leaving Ecuador with nothing but hope and determination could create a life filled with opportunity, meaning, and purpose. It was proof that courage, when combined with persistence, could transform uncertainty into stability and dreams into reality.

As the final words of the oath settled in the room, Miguel felt a grounding clarity. It was not triumph alone, but a quiet acceptance of new responsibility—the awareness that becoming part of a country also meant contributing to its story. That realization gave the moment a solemn beauty, reminding him that belonging is shaped not only by place, but by participation, effort, and intention.

For Miguel, this milestone was not only about himself. It was a gift to those who would follow, his children, his family, and even the countless friends and neighbors whose lives intertwined with his along the way. Citizenship was a lesson, a beacon, and a symbol of what dedication and faith can achieve.

Even after the ceremony, Miguel reflected on what it truly meant to belong. Being American, he realized, did not erase where he came from. His roots, his childhood in Guayaquil, the streets where he first ran, the schools he walked to barefoot—all of it remained. Citizenship did not replace those memories; it added to them, blending the past with the present, shaping the life he had built for himself and for his family.

He remembered the long bus rides across Central America, the faces of strangers who had offered him kindness, and the moments of fear when the journey seemed impossible. Each memory became a thread woven into the tapestry of his life, teaching resilience, humility, and empathy. The oath he recited reflected all those steps, both big and small.

Afterward, Miguel and Maria celebrated quietly in a small diner near their apartment. Two slices of cheesecake, two cups of coffee, and the snow falling outside the window seemed to make the ordinary feel monumental. They spoke softly, reflecting on how far they had come together—from the streets of Guayaquil to the avenues of New York, from youthful dreams to tangible achievement.

"Hiciste bien, hijo," Maria said, her voice full of pride (*You did well, son*).

"Gracias, mami, ahora soy un Americano," Miguel replied, a quiet smile spreading across his face (*Thank you, mom, now I'm an American*).

That night, as he returned to their modest apartment, Miguel looked around and realized something profound. Home is not simply a place, a set of walls, or a neighborhood. Home is built slowly, piece by piece, by the choices we make, the people we love, and the values we hold dear. Home is courage in the face of fear, persistence when times are uncertain, and hope that tomorrow can be better than today.

Miguel's journey to citizenship reminds us that immigration is an act of bravery, not just logistics. It is leaving everything familiar behind—the language, the culture, the streets that shaped you—to embrace a future unknown. And yet, it is in that very act of leaving that life can transform, that dreams can take root, and that ordinary people can achieve extraordinary outcomes.

He taught us that courage is not always loud. It is quiet, consistent, and often invisible to the outside world. It is found in waking up every day to build a life, to face challenges, and to create possibilities for oneself and for those who follow. Miguel's citizenship was one of many steps, but it was also a milestone that encapsulated a lifetime of quiet determination and steady faith. By looking back at his journey, we see the universality of his story. It is a story of hope for every immigrant who dreams of building something new, for every person who dares to leave behind what they know to pursue what they can become. It is proof that success is possible, that dreams are valid, and that the human spirit can thrive even in unfamiliar, challenging lands.

Citizenship became a lens through which Miguel viewed life—a reminder of what is possible when one is willing to act with courage, integrity, and perseverance. It marked a beginning, not an end. It was a reminder that every decision, every risk, and every effort has the power to shape not only a life, but a legacy. In the days that followed, Miguel noticed how the world around him felt subtly different—not because the streets had changed, but because his relationship to them had. Everyday scenes carried new meaning, and the ordinary details became reminders that he had woven himself into the fabric of a new home, one choice and one year at a time.

As snow continued to fall outside their apartment that night, Miguel sat quietly, reflecting on the journey that had brought him to that moment. The path had been long and sometimes lonely. It had required patience, faith, and the belief that leaving home could lead to something better. And in the quiet, he understood: the life he had built, the family he loved, and the legacy he would leave behind were all proof that courage and hope were worth every step.

11
Later Adventures and Reflections

Even after building a life in New York, raising a family, and becoming an American citizen, Miguel's love for exploration never faded. Travel remained a constant thread in his life—a way to learn, grow, and experience the world firsthand. He returned to Europe often, revisiting cities like Italy, France, and Spain, finding both familiar comforts and new adventures in every journey. The streets of Rome, the canals of Venice, and the cafés of Paris became places of reflection, curiosity, and discovery.

Miguel also explored parts of Latin America and the Caribbean, embracing the rich cultures, languages, and histories that reminded him of home. Each trip offered lessons—patience when navigating unfamiliar places, humility when learning from new people, and wonder at the beauty of landscapes and human connection alike.

Even in his travels, Miguel always found humor and joy in small, unexpected moments. He recounted the time he got lost in a bustling European market, only to find himself sharing a table with strangers who became friends by the end of the day. He laughed at his mispronunciations in foreign languages, delighted in tasting new foods, and cherished every chance to learn something different from someone's perspective. These stories, small yet meaningful, reflected a man who embraced life fully—curious, adventurous, and open-hearted.

Back in New York, Miguel balanced his worldly experiences with his responsibilities at home. He continued working, contributing to his community, and sharing his insights with those around him. He demonstrated that a fulfilling life doesn't require extremes, but a commitment to growth, curiosity, and embracing the opportunities life offers.

Through work, travel, and friendships, Miguel exemplified the fullness of life: the harmony between stability and adventure, between responsibilities and personal joy. He taught those around him—especially his children—that life is richest when approached with an open mind, a courageous heart, and a willingness to explore the unknown.

12
Reencuentro — Coming Full Circle

A Daughter's Perspective

When I was growing up, I always imagined what it would have been like for my father to see Ecuador again after all those years away—to walk through the streets of his childhood, to feel the air he once breathed as a young man with dreams in his pocket. He used to tell me stories about Guido, his closest friend, the one who stayed behind when he left. So, when my father finally made that trip back years later, I think it meant more than even he could put into words. What follows is how I imagine that reunion—a reflection of what home truly means.

❧

It had been more than three decades since Miguel had last set foot in Ecuador.

Time had moved swiftly, carrying him across oceans and through countless memories, but now, as the plane descended into Guayaquil, he felt something stir deep inside him—a quiet trembling of recognition.

The same humid air that once greeted him as a young man now wrapped around him again, warm and familiar.

He looked out the window, seeing the city lights glittering like scattered stars. So much had changed—new roads, new buildings, a skyline that looked taller—yet beneath it all, there was still the heartbeat of the place that had shaped him.

Stepping off the plane, he inhaled deeply. The scent of the sea breeze mixed with faint exhaust fumes and roasted corn from a nearby vendor. It was a scent he hadn't realized he'd missed until now. For a moment, Miguel simply stood still, letting the sounds of the airport wash over him—announcements echoing overhead, suitcases rolling across tile, voices layered in accents he had not heard in decades. Each sound tugged at an old memory.

He had returned not only to visit family but also to reconnect with someone who had been part of his story from the very beginning—his old friend, Guido.

For the last time they had seen each other, they were barely nineteen, standing on a dusty road near the border of Colombia, two boys trying to become men. Miguel had chosen to continue north. Guido had turned back. For years, Miguel had wondered what became of him. He wondered whether Guido would recognize him at all, or if time had reshaped them both beyond familiarity. He felt the weight of all the years that had passed—years filled with choices, distances, and moments neither could explain to the other. Yet beneath the uncertainty was a quiet hope that some bonds survive even long silence.

The reunion took place on a warm Sunday afternoon near the Malecón 2000, Guayaquil's reimagined waterfront. The sun shimmered on the Guayas River, and the soft hum of laughter, music, and conversation floated in the air. Miguel arrived early, his heart beating with anticipation.

He spotted Guido before Guido saw him—sitting on a bench beneath a palm tree, wearing a Panama hat and reading glasses, his face lined with time but his eyes unmistakably the same.

For a moment, Miguel hesitated. How do you greet someone who was part of the most defining chapter of your life?

Then Guido looked up—and smiled.

"Miguel… ¡no puede ser!" Guido's voice cracked as he stood, his arms opening in disbelief and joy (*Miguel… it can't be).*

Miguel laughed, his throat tight as he said, "Sí, hermano… soy yo" (*Yes, brother… it's me*).

The two men embraced tightly, the years melting away in an instant. Around them, the city buzzed on, but for Miguel and Guido, time stood still.

They spent the afternoon walking along the riverfront, talking as if no time had passed. Guido had remained in Ecuador, married, raised children, and built a quiet life as a teacher. He spoke proudly of his grandchildren, of his small home, of the mango trees in his yard.

"Y tú," Guido said with a playful grin, "tú sí lo lograste. Siempre supe que lo harías" (*And you—you actually made it. I always knew you would*).

Miguel smiled and said, "No fue fácil, pero valió la pena. Encontré una vida nueva… una que ni siquiera sabía que buscaba" (*It wasn't easy, but it was worth it. I found a new life… one I didn't even know I was searching for*).

Guido nodded thoughtfully. "A veces me preguntaba qué habría sido de ti. Cuando escuchaba hablar de América, te imaginaba caminando por las calles de Nueva York, mirando esos edificios gigantes" (*Sometimes I wondered what became of you. When I'd hear about America, I pictured you walking through the streets of New York, staring up at those giant buildings*).

Miguel chuckled. "Eso fue exactamente lo que hice la primera semana. No podía dejar de mirar hacia arriba" (*That's exactly what I did the first week. I couldn't stop looking up*).

They laughed together, their voices carried with the breeze.

After a pause, Guido's tone softened. "Sabes, a veces me sentía culpable por no haber ido contigo" (*You know, sometimes I felt guilty for not going with you*).

Miguel stopped walking and looked at him as he said, "No sientas eso. Tomaste el camino que era correcto para ti. Los dos lo hicimos" (*Don't feel that way. You chose what was right for you. We both did*).

Guido exhaled slowly, his gaze lost on the river. "Tal vez. Pero siempre me pregunté si me perdí de algo" (*Maybe. Still, I always wondered if I missed something*).

"No te perdiste nada," Miguel said gently. "Encontraste tu hogar aquí. Y yo encontré el mío allá. Eso es todo lo que la vida nos pide" (*You didn't miss anything. You found your home here. And I found mine there. That's all life really asks of us*).

As the sun began to set, painting the sky in shades of rose and amber, they sat on the same bench where they had first met that afternoon. Children played nearby, vendors called out their last sales of the day, and music drifted from a radio somewhere behind them—an old bolero that carried the weight of nostalgia.

"¿Alguna vez piensas," Guido asked quietly, "que todo salió exactamente como debía salir?" (*Do you ever think that everything turned out exactly as it was meant to?*).

Miguel nodded, smiling faintly as he said, "Todos los días" (*Every day*).

They sat in silence, the kind of silence that doesn't need to be filled. The years of distance, the unspoken memories, the what-ifs—all of it seemed to fade under the warm Ecuadorian sun.

When it was time to part, Miguel stood and took a long look at the city around him—the city that had once been home, and in a way, always would be.

"Cuídate, Guido" (*Take care of yourself, Guido*).

"Y tú, hermano," Guido said, smiling. "No esperes otros mas años para volver" (*And you, brother. Don't wait many years to come back*).

Miguel smiled and said, "Lo intentaré" (*I'll try*).

They hugged again, holding onto each other just a second longer than before—an embrace of gratitude, forgiveness, and peace.

As Miguel walked away, he glanced over his shoulder. Guido was still standing by the bench, waving, the golden light of sunset catching his face.

In that moment, Miguel realized something: home wasn't a place. It wasn't New York or Guayaquil. It was the feeling of belonging—the sense of having lived truly and fully, of finding peace in where life had led you.

He had left Ecuador chasing a dream.

Now, he returned not to reclaim something lost—but to honor everything he had found.

Everything had worked out exactly as it was meant to.

He had found his home.

And so, had Guido.

A Daughter's Reflection

When my father told me about seeing Guido again, there was a quiet glow in his eyes—not just of happiness, but of peace. I think that reunion reminded him that success isn't measured by where you end up, but by how far you've come and the people who shaped you along the way. Hearing his story made me realize that "home" isn't a destination. It's the heart you carry—one that always knows where it came from and who walked beside it.

13
Two Homes, One Heart

The days in Ecuador passed gently, like the unhurried rhythm of a familiar song. Miguel spent his mornings walking through the old neighborhoods, tracing steps he once took as a boy. Every corner carried a memory—a story waiting to be remembered.

There was a quiet familiarity in the way the morning unfolded—vendors setting up their stands, the distant hum of motorcycles, the call of street-sellers drifting across the neighborhood. These ordinary sounds wrapped around him like a rhythm he had known long before he learned the cadence of New York.

He stood outside the small house where he was born, now repainted in brighter colors. The walls were thinner than he remembered, the street narrower, the trees taller. Children ran past him, laughing in the same carefree way he once did. He smiled. Time had moved forward, but the essence of life here hadn't changed—the same warmth, the same simplicity, the same unbreakable spirit.

He visited old family friends who still lived nearby, women who remembered him as el niño curioso, the curious boy who always asked questions. They served him coffee and pan de yuca, eager to hear about his adventures in America.

"Nunca te olvidaste de dónde vienes, ¿verdad?" one of them asked (*You never forgot where you came from, did you?*).

Miguel shook his head, smiling softly as he said, "No, señora. Eso nunca se olvida" (*No, ma'am. You never forget that*).

But as the days passed, he also felt something deeper stirring inside him—a quiet realization that the life he once longed for here no longer belonged to him. The rhythm of Ecuador was comforting, but his own rhythm had changed. He had spent too many years in motion—living, learning, and building a home across the ocean.

At night, lying in his childhood room, he thought about his younger self—the nineteen-year-old who had set out with a backpack, a passport, and a dream. He remembered the fear, the exhaustion, the nights spent wondering if he'd ever make it. He also remembered the laughter, the people who helped him along the way, and the strength that kept him going.

Ecuador had taught him how to dream.

America had taught him how to live those dreams.

He realized now that both places held pieces of him—one in his past, and one in his present.

As the final days approached, he found himself lingering a little longer in each place he visited, letting the textures and colors settle into memory. He wasn't trying to hold on—he was simply acknowledging what this land had given him, and how it had shaped every step that followed.

Before his flight back to New York, Miguel took one last walk along the Malecón.

The afternoon sun shimmered on the river like liquid gold, and a soft breeze carried the scent of salt and flowers. He paused for a moment, closing his eyes.

"Gracias," he whispered, his voice steady but emotional (*Thank you*).

It wasn't just gratitude to Ecuador, but to the life it had given him—the foundation of his courage, the roots that kept him grounded no matter how far he traveled.

The next morning, as the plane lifted off the runway, Miguel looked down at the land disappearing below—the winding rivers, the mountains fading into clouds, the endless green of the countryside. He thought of Guido, of his family, of every road that had led him here.

He was filled not with sadness, but peace. Ecuador would always be part of him, but his heart now beat to the pulse of another city—one of chaos and noise and movement, one that had given him everything he had once dreamed of.

By the time the plane touched down in New York, the sun was setting. The sky outside was streaked with pink and orange, like a promise of homecoming.

As he walked through the airport, his steps quickened. He took a cab home, counting the minutes down to when he was home. And then he saw her—his mother, Maria, standing near the kitchen, waving just like she had all those years ago when he first arrived.

Her hair was shorter, now, her steps slower, but her smile—that same radiant smile—was unchanged.

Miguel dropped his suitcase and hurried forward. For a brief second, he felt like the young man who had first arrived in this country—uncertain, hopeful, desperate to see the one familiar face that meant safety. Even after all these years, that feeling rose again, warm and immediate.

Maria opened her arms, and when they hugged, it felt like every mile between Ecuador and New York disappeared.

"Mijo," she whispered tearfully, "sabía que volverías" (*My son, I knew you'd come back*).

Miguel laughed softly against her shoulder as he said, "Siempre vuelvo, mami" (*I always come back, mami*).

They stood there, holding onto each other as people passed by, the noise of the airport fading into the background. In that embrace, Miguel realized that while his journey had taken him across countries and oceans, his destination had always been the same—here, in the arms of his mother, in the place where he had built his life.

He didn't have to choose between Ecuador and America anymore. He carried both within him—one as his beginning, the other as his becoming.

That night, back in his apartment, Miguel unpacked his suitcase. He placed a small souvenir from Ecuador—a carved wooden figure of the Virgen del Cisne—on his bookshelf beside photos of his travels, his children, and his mother.

Looking around, he felt a deep sense of contentment. The walls were filled with memories, the air with warmth.

He whispered to himself, almost like a prayer:

"Dos hogares. Un corazón" (*Two homes. One heart*).

And with that, he knew—the journey that began so many years ago had finally come full circle.

14
A Journey Home

For Miguel, traveling was never just about seeing new places—it was about rediscovering parts of himself along the way. From the moment he first left Ecuador as a young man, he carried within him a curiosity that never faded. Each new country, each city, each fleeting encounter left an imprint on him, reminding him how vast and beautiful the world could be.

But of all his journeys, there was one that meant more than any other: the one that brought him back home.

Years had passed since Miguel last saw Ecuador. Life in New York had kept him busy—working, raising a family, and building a life that reflected everything he had once dreamed of. Yet even after all that time, Ecuador was never far from his heart.

Then came the loss that changed everything. When Maria, his beloved mother, passed away, it left a quiet space in his heart that no amount of travel or success could fill. She had been his anchor—the one who first welcomed him to America, who held his hand through the subway tunnels, who smiled at the sight of her son finally home after years apart.

Her passing reminded him just how deeply his roots ran, not only in New York but also in the soil of the land he once called home.

After years of waiting—and after the long stillness brought by the pandemic—the family finally decided it was time to return to Ecuador together. It had been decades since Miguel had last walked those streets, and now, he would do so surrounded by his children, carrying the memory of Maria in his heart.

It was not a simple vacation. It was a journey of remembrance—of honoring where everything began, and the woman who made it all possible.

When the plane descended over the Andes, the view took everyone's breath away.

The air on the tarmac smelled of earth and sun-warmed grass; distant church bells threaded through the chatter of families reuniting. For a moment, the world felt immediate, color, sound, heat, as if every memory had a smell and every step could unlock one.

The mountains rose like waves of green and gold, the valleys shimmering in the sunlight. Miguel stared out the window, his eyes distant, reflecting both joy and melancholy.

"Mira eso," he said softly. "Look at that. It's even more beautiful than I remembered."

The moment they stepped onto Ecuadorian soil, something shifted in him. The warmth of the air, the smell of the food, the music playing faintly in the distance—it all came rushing back.

He closed his eyes and let himself notice the small things: the cadence of the language around him, the tug of humidity on his shirt, a vendor calling a fruit by the old name. It wasn't flashback or regret, it was a gentle reconnection, like finding an old rhythm you'd only half-remembered.

He smiled quietly, taking it all in, his children watching with admiration and understanding.

"Your abuela walked these streets," he said, pointing down a narrow road lined with colorful houses. "This is where it all began."

The family spent days exploring—visiting the coastal city of Guayaquil, where Miguel was born, the markets alive with sound and color, the rivers that once shaped his childhood. He showed them the school he had attended, the parks where he used to play, and the churches where Maria once prayed for their safety when he first left for America.

Every step of the trip carried her memory.

At one point, they visited a quiet overlook above the city. The view stretched endlessly—a sea of rooftops under a blazing sunset. Miguel stood there for a long moment, the wind gently lifting his hair.

"She would have loved this," he said softly.

No one needed to ask who "she" was.

It wasn't just nostalgia that filled the trip; it was gratitude. Miguel walked through Ecuador not as the young man chasing dreams anymore, but as someone who had lived them—who had built a life, raised children, and carried forward his mother's strength and faith.

His children saw him differently now. They saw the young traveler who once crossed borders with nothing but courage. They watched him point to an alleyway, then listen with a hush as an elder told a joke in rapid Spanish; in those small exchanges, they read a history they hadn't known—not a legend, but a lived, ordinary bravery. The children's admiration was quiet and practical: a look that said, I understand a little more now.

They saw the man who became their father, who built a home out of hope and hard work.

Together, they laughed, shared meals, and listened to stories they had never heard before, about Miguel's adventures, his first jobs, and the funny moments that shaped his early years in America.

"You see," he told them one night over dinner, "dreams don't have to be perfect. They just have to be yours."

When the time came to leave Ecuador, there was a quiet understanding among them all. The trip had brought them closer—not just to each other, but to their heritage, to Maria, and to the journey that started it all.

At the airport, Miguel looked out the window once more, watching the landscape disappear beneath the clouds. He smiled—not with sadness, but with peace.

"Estoy listo," he said softly (*I'm ready*).

The children understood. Ecuador would always be part of him, but New York was where he had built his life—where Maria had once waited for him at the station, where he had raised his children, and where his dreams had truly taken root.

When they arrived back in New York, it felt different somehow. The air was the same, the skyline unchanged, but their hearts carried something new—a deeper sense of belonging.

In that journey back and forth, the circle had quietly completed itself.

Miguel had left Ecuador to find a future, and decades later, he returned—not alone, not uncertain, but surrounded by the family that his courage had made possible.

And though Maria was gone, her spirit was present in every laugh, every shared meal, every step they took. She had been the first to show Miguel the meaning of home, and now, through him, that meaning had passed to a new generation.

A Daughter's Reflection

Sometimes, home isn't a single place. It's a feeling you carry—in your memories, in your family, in the stories that outlive you. For Miguel, home was both Ecuador and New York. It was the past that shaped him and the present that sustained him.

And for us, his children, that journey taught us that no matter how far we travel, we always carry a piece of our roots within us—the courage, the sacrifice, and the love that began long before we were even born.

15
Legacy and Inspiration

Miguel's life continues to be more than a story of immigration, travel, or professional achievement. It is a story of values, determination, and the quiet courage that allows ordinary people to achieve extraordinary things—a story that is still being written every day.

His journey—from Ecuador to New York, through adventures around the globe, and into citizenship, parenthood, and family life—remains a testament to perseverance, independence, and curiosity. It shows that life can be full and meaningful, even amid ordinary challenges, and that the power of dreams lies in the willingness to pursue them.

As a father, he teaches lessons that are simple yet profound: work hard, follow your dreams, trust yourself, and embrace every opportunity to learn and grow. Courage, he shows, isn't always dramatic; it can be quiet, steady, and persistent. His example continues to guide us, shaping the way we view our own possibilities, ambitions, and approaches to challenges.

Even in ordinary moments—a shared meal, a trip together, a conversation late at night—Miguel leaves subtle but powerful marks on those around him. I remember our first trip together to Ecuador, years after he had left. Seeing him walk through the streets of Guayaquil again, pointing out corners where he had played as a boy, and explaining the neighborhoods where his family had struggled and thrived—it was like watching history come alive.

He shared stories I had only heard in fragments, and I realized that his courage shapes not only his life but ours as well. Watching him there, slow, soft, content, the kids saw the man behind the stories: not a myth, but someone who had kept pieces of home with him and was finally showing them.

Though this story is told from my perspective, it is clear that his influence reaches far beyond our family. Miguel reminds anyone who spends time with him that ordinary people can achieve remarkable things, that independence and exploration are invaluable, and that perseverance, curiosity, and courage are keys to creating a meaningful life.

Influence, in his case, looked like practical help and consistent kindness, not grand gestures.

Even after my grandmother Maria passed and the pandemic made travel difficult, we finally returned to Ecuador together as a family. Watching my father's eyes light up as he introduced us to his old neighborhoods, childhood friends, and the landscapes that shaped him, I understood something essential: home is both where you start and where you create your life. We honored Maria's memory in those moments, remembering everything she stood for and all the sacrifices she made to give him opportunities. Those memories continue to shape our family story, bridging past and present.

Miguel's life may not always be filled with dramatic peril or harrowing adventure, but it is full of heart, hope, and possibility. He demonstrates that courage doesn't always roar; sometimes it whispers quietly, guiding us forward. In the quiet courage of his everyday life, we see a life lived fully—a life that inspires, teaches, and reminds us that the possibilities before us are endless when we step forward with intention.

As his daughter, I carry his lessons forward in my own life—in the way I work, explore, and nurture relationships. By sharing our experiences together, I honor the ongoing acts of courage, perseverance, and love that define his life. Miguel's story is living proof that the impact of one person—guided by integrity, love, and determination—can ripple across generations.

And so, the story does not end here. It continues in the lives of those he touches, in the dreams we pursue, and in the courage we summon to make our own paths. Miguel shows us that home is not just a place—it is a journey, a vision, and a legacy carried forward by those willing to follow it.

As this chapter closes, the story remains ours—a story to remember, a story to cherish, and a story to continue writing together. Miguel's life reminds us of one simple truth: the life you dream of is possible, the courage to pursue it is within you, and the legacy you leave behind is measured not by what you take, but by what you give—every single day.

16
Reflections on a Life Well Lived

As I write these words, I find myself thinking not only about the life my father has already led, but about the way he continues to shape our family, and our understanding of the world. Miguel's story—the boy who left Ecuador with little more than hope, the man who built a life in New York, the father who teaches courage, perseverance, and curiosity—is more than a tale of travel, immigration, or achievement. It is a story of heart, values, and the quiet acts that define a life well-lived.

I still remember the first time he took my relatives and me on a long drive around New York. The sun was setting, painting the skyline in shades of gold and amber, and he pointed to the skyline with a smile that seemed to hold both pride and promise.

"Everything you see," he said, "is possible if you work for it, if you are brave enough to take the first step."

Even as a child, I felt the weight of those words—not as pressure, but as an invitation. An invitation to explore, to dream, and to act.

Years later, we returned to Ecuador together as a family. Seeing him walk the streets, the scent of fresh bread from local bakeries mingled with the earthy aroma of rain on cobblestones, and I noticed how his face softened, a mixture of nostalgia and pride. He spoke softly of the hardships he endured, of lessons learned in struggle, and of the beauty he always carried in his heart for his homeland. Yet, as much as he loves Ecuador, he has never stopped cherishing the life he has built in New York—a life that allows him to provide for his family, explore the world, and share new experiences with us.

During that trip, we laughed, cried, and remembered. We visited old friends, walked along the streets he once roamed as a boy, and even ate at the same small bakery he had loved as a child. At one point, he paused, staring at a familiar corner of Quito.

"You know," he said, "home isn't only where you were born. Home is where you live, where you love, and where you leave a piece of yourself."

His lessons extend beyond words. In the kitchen, he teaches patience, showing us that cooking is not just about ingredients, but about care and intention—the slow stirring of a pot, the aroma of spices filling the air, the rhythm of chopping that becomes almost meditative. In his work, he demonstrates discipline and curiosity, proving that even small, consistent effort can yield extraordinary results. And in travel, he shows the joy of seeing the world while carrying your roots with you.

Even now, Miguel's life is full of adventures—not always in distant countries, but in the small moments that make life rich. We often joke about his endless lists of places he wants to see, yet he never rushes. He savors each step, each conversation, and each quiet morning. He finds meaning not in speed, but in presence.

One evening, after a long day exploring Ecuador, we sat on a balcony overlooking the city. He told stories of his childhood, of the struggles he faced, and of the courage it took to leave everything familiar behind.

My relatives and I listened, fascinated not by the hardships alone, but by the calm, steady strength with which he faced them. I realized then that his courage was not the dramatic, flashy kind you read about in books—it was the quiet, persistent courage of living fully, thoughtfully, and with intention.

At home in New York, Miguel continues to lead by example. He reminds us that dreams are not always immediate, that progress often comes in small, steady steps, and that resilience is built not in moments of triumph, but in the quiet persistence of daily choices. I see his influence in every decision I make, every challenge I face, and every joy I embrace. Miguel isn't perfect, just like none of us are. We are all human, and we make mistakes. But he has taught me that every day is a gift. He's shown me how to live with gratitude, kindness, and respect, no matter what obstacles lie ahead. We can't change the past, but we can change our present and future.

Writing this chapter is my way of honoring him—capturing not just the events of his life, but the values, faith, and courage that continue to guide him and our family. He shows us that independence, perseverance, and curiosity are not only possible but transformative. And perhaps the most important lesson he teaches is this: courage is often quiet. It is in the small steps we take toward our dreams, the decisions we make with integrity, and the love we give freely.

Miguel's journey is far from over. Each day, he embraces life with heart, intention, and joy. He travels, he teaches, he loves, and he dreams—reminding us all that ordinary beginnings can lead to extraordinary outcomes. For all of us, he demonstrates that life, when embraced fully, is a gift to explore, cherish, and share.

And in that truth, I find gratitude, admiration, and hope—for my father, for our family, and for everyone inspired to follow their own journey, wherever it may lead.

17
The Journey Worth Taking

Immigration is a decision unlike any other. It asks of us a courage that is often silent, a faith that must persist even when hope seems uncertain, and a willingness to embrace a life utterly unknown. It is a choice that tests the limits of our spirit, yet also illuminates the capacity for growth that exists in every person willing to step into the unknown.

To leave the place that shaped you—the streets where you learned your first lessons, the family and friends who are the foundation of your early life, the familiar sounds, smells, and rhythms that define "home" —is not a choice made lightly. And yet, for so many, including countless men and women before us, it is a choice that promises transformation, possibility, and, ultimately, fulfillment.

I have watched this truth unfold in the life of my father, Miguel. He chose, in his youth, to leave behind everything he had ever known in Ecuador and step into the uncertainty of the United States. He carried little more than hope and determination, yet that act of bravery became the seed from which a remarkable life would grow. There is a lesson here, one that transcends geography, culture, and circumstance: that courage to start anew, when directed by purpose and love, can change not only the life of the individual but the lives of generations to come.

Leaving home is always accompanied by doubt. It is accompanied by fear. It is accompanied by longing— longing for familiar streets, for the smell of a favorite meal, for voices that have always felt like safety. These feelings, while heavy in the moment, are the very forge in which resilience and character are shaped, preparing the traveler for the life that awaits beyond fear.

Anyone who has embarked on this journey knows the weight of those emotions. They press on the heart in quiet, persistent ways. There are nights when one wonders if the choice was right, mornings when hope feels fragile, and moments when the unfamiliar seems insurmountable. And yet, to endure those feelings, to move forward despite them, is to take the first step into possibility.

Immigration, at its core, is a statement of faith. It is the acknowledgment that the life you have now is not the life you are destined to have. It is the declaration that your story is not finished and that a broader, fuller, richer story awaits—one that can encompass dreams you have not yet dared to imagine. My father's journey illustrates this perfectly. The roads were not always smooth. The nights were long, and the struggles were many. He faced uncertainty, loneliness, and obstacles that could have easily ended his hopes. Yet, each step forward was guided by the vision of a better life, a life where he could provide, grow, and leave a legacy for his children.

This is the beauty of the immigrant journey: it transforms ordinary courage into extraordinary outcomes. When someone leaves home to seek opportunity, they are not only claiming a chance for themselves; they are claiming a future for those who will come after them. They are rewriting the possibilities of their family, their community, and even the world in small, powerful ways. The ripple effect of such a choice is immeasurable. A decision made in the quiet of one person's heart can reverberate through generations.

There is a certain alchemy to this process. Hardship, sacrifice, and uncertainty, though heavy and often painful, are the elements through which resilience is forged. They teach patience, creativity, humility, and gratitude. My father learned that each day, each challenge, each small victory was a piece of the life he was building—one that would eventually support dreams, ambitions, and stability far beyond what he had imagined as a young man in Ecuador. In this way, the journey of immigration is also a journey of becoming: becoming stronger, wiser, more compassionate, and more capable of embracing the world on one's own terms.

Yet, the journey is never simply about survival. It is about transformation. Immigrants do not merely leave behind what they know; they take with them what they are, and they shape it into something new. Values, traditions, lessons from childhood—these travel quietly in the heart, and they merge with new experiences, new languages, and new ways of seeing the world. The immigrant builds a bridge between the past and the future, between the familiar and the unknown. That bridge becomes not just a pathway, but a foundation for life.

In reflecting on this, it is clear that immigration is not without its moments of pain. Separation from family, nostalgia for a homeland, the ache of cultural displacement—these are realities that anyone who has left home must face. But these challenges, as difficult as they are, are also the crucible in which courage is tempered. They teach perspective. They teach resilience. They teach that the sacrifices made today are not losses but investments in the promise of tomorrow.

What makes an immigrant's journey truly remarkable is the duality of its nature: to leave is to risk, but to arrive—and to build—is to claim victory. Each decision, each small act of courage, lays stones in a path that others will follow, turning personal triumph into collective inheritance.

Miguel's life is an embodiment of this duality. He arrived in a new country with nothing but hope and determination. He moved through a string of jobs—long factory shifts marked by exhaustion, stress, and hardship—enduring both physical and emotional strain to build a new life for his family. Through persistence, hard work, and unwavering commitment, he became the foundation of a family, a source of inspiration, and a symbol of what it means to turn courage into success. The rewards of his journey were not immediate, but they were profound and enduring.

This is the message I hope every reader takes to heart: that the challenges of starting anew, no matter how daunting, are worth the risk. To leave what is familiar, to face the unknown, to embrace the possibility of failure—these are not acts of recklessness but of profound bravery. And in that bravery lies the opportunity to create a life that is meaningful, not only for oneself but for those who follow. The immigrant's path is one of both personal growth and collective legacy. Each decision, each step forward, contributes to a story that is greater than any one individual.

And so, the act of immigration becomes more than a relocation. It becomes an assertion of hope. It becomes a statement of belief—belief in the possibility of a better life, belief in the capacity of oneself to endure and thrive, and belief in the responsibility one carries to future generations. It is the quiet heroism of everyday choices that propels families, communities, and nations forward.

Through this lens, success is redefined. It is not measured solely by wealth, status, or acclaim. It is measured by the impact of one's decisions, the courage to pursue possibilities, and the dedication to leave the world—or at least one's family—in a better place than it was found. Success can be seen in a home filled with love, in a child encouraged to dream, or in the preservation of traditions that might otherwise be forgotten—quiet, yet profound markers of a life well-lived.

For immigrants, this success often manifests in ways that are subtle yet powerful: a child who graduates from school, a parent who provides stability, a home that embodies love and care, a tradition preserved, a dream realized. These are the quiet victories that matter most.

In reflecting on Miguel's life, I am reminded of the infinite ways courage and vision can shape the course of a life. The journey was never easy, and the obstacles were numerous, yet each choice to continue forward—each embrace of uncertainty—became a step toward fulfillment. The life he built stands as a testament not just to what one man can accomplish but to what is possible when fear is met with determination, when hope is met with action, and when love is the compass guiding each decision.

Immigration is, ultimately, an act of hope made tangible. It is the embodiment of faith in oneself and in the possibilities of life. Those who choose this path demonstrate the remarkable capacity of the human spirit: to dream, to endure, to create, and to flourish even in the face of uncertainty. Their stories illuminate the profound truth that a life of courage, commitment, and purpose can emerge from the simplest of beginnings—a suitcase, a letter from a loved one, and a heart full of hope.

And for those who follow, the lessons are clear: bravery in leaving is only the first step. Perseverance, integrity, and love must follow. Hard work, patience, and reflection shape the journey. And, most importantly, the rewards—though not immediate—are enduring. To become the face of success in your family, to provide opportunities for those who come after you, to embody the values you hold dear—these are the true outcomes of a life devoted to the immigrant's path.

This book, in its essence, is an homage to all who have taken such a path. It is a reflection on the power of courage, on the endurance of hope, and on the quiet ways ordinary people transform their families and communities. It is a reminder that the act of leaving is itself an act of creation—creating opportunity, creating a home, creating a story that others will carry forward.

If there is a single truth to take away, it is this: the challenges faced along the journey are not signs that the path is wrong, but evidence that it is meaningful. Every fear confronted, every obstacle overcome, every step taken toward the unknown strengthens the foundation of a life well-lived. And when that life becomes the foundation for others, its impact echoes far beyond what the traveler could ever imagine.

Immigration is a story of courage. It is a story of transformation. It is a story of love, for oneself, for one's family, and for the future. And in reflecting on my father's journey, I am reminded that ordinary choices, made with heart and conviction, can lead to extraordinary outcomes. That the decision to leave, to embrace the unknown, and to build anew is one of the most profound acts of human courage.

As this story ends, it is clear that the journey of migration is more than a physical movement. It is the pursuit of hope, the shaping of character, and the creation of a legacy. To take the first step is to believe in the unseen, to trust in one's capacity to grow, and to commit to the work of building a life that honors both past and future.

For Miguel, for all who have taken similar paths, and for those who will follow, the truth remains: courage may be quiet, success may be humble, and the journey may be filled with doubt. Yet the act of stepping forward, of leaving behind the known, and of embracing the unknown, can yield a life more remarkable than anyone could have imagined. It is a reminder to us all that courage, however quiet, when guided by purpose and love, can transform not just a life, but the lives of everyone touched by it.

This is the essence of immigration: the willingness to dream, the courage to act, and the determination to shape a life worth living. It is a lesson in resilience, in hope, and in love. And it is a lesson that, once understood, resonates far beyond one story, one family, or one life.

It is a message for all who seek to transform their world, to build a future, and to become the living proof that extraordinary outcomes arise from ordinary beginnings. May it inspire each of us to take our own first steps into the unknown, trusting that even the smallest choices can blossom into legacies that endure.

Thank you for joining us on this beautiful journey, we wish you all the absolute best (*Gracias, por acompañarnos en este hermoso viaje, les deseamos todo lo mejor*).